Creepy Crafts & MORE
MONSTERS

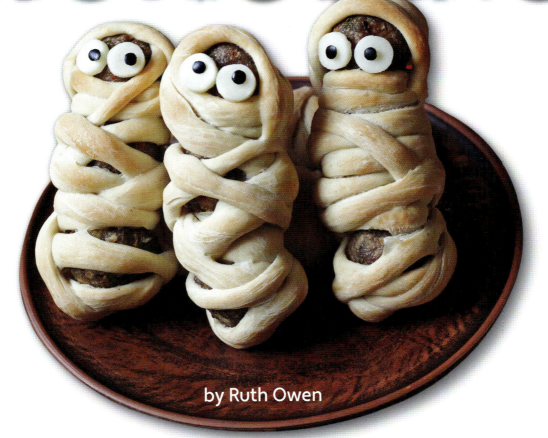

by Ruth Owen

Minneapolis, Minnesota

Credits

Cover, © Shutterstock; 1, © Shutterstock; 3, © Ase/Shutterstock and © Ruth Owen Books; 4, © Ruth Owen Books; 5, © Shutterstock and © Ruth Owen Books; 6, © leolintang/Shutterstock and © Ruth Owen Books; 7, © Ruth Owen Books; 8–9, © Ruth Owen Books; 10, © Ase/Shutterstock and © Ruth Owen Books; 11, © Shutterstock and © Ruth Owen Books; 12–13, © Ruth Owen Books; 14, © GreenArt/Shutterstock; 15, © Shutterstock and © Ruth Owen Books; 16–17, © Ruth Owen Books; 18, © Kjpargeter/Shutterstock, © Kathy Hutchins/Shutterstock, and © Ruth Owen Books; 19, © Ruth Owen Books; 20T, © jonnysek-jiri/Shutterstock; 20–21, © Ruth Owen Books; 22L, © Kathy Hutchins/Shutterstock; 22TR, © Photononstop/Superstock; 22BR, © Zacarias Pereira da Mata/Shutterstock; 23TL, © ANGHI/Shutterstock; 23BL, © Andrea Izzotti/Shutterstock; 23TR, © Sarymsakov Andrey/Shutterstock; 23BR, © WitR/Shutterstock.

Photo Researcher: Ruth Owen Books with photography by Charles Francis

Library of Congress Cataloging-in-Publication Data

Names: Owen, Ruth, 1967- author.
Title: Monsters / by Ruth Owen.
Description: Create! | Minneapolis, Minnesota : Bearport Publishing
   Company, [2021] | Series: Creepy crafts & more | Includes
   bibliographical references and index.
Identifiers: LCCN 2020006092 (print) | LCCN 2020006093 (ebook) |
   ISBN 9781647471873 (library binding) | ISBN 9781647471941 (ebook)
Subjects: LCSH: Handicraft–Juvenile literature. | Monsters–Juvenile
   literature. | Food in art–Juvenile literature.
Classification: LCC TT160 .O8444 2021 (print) | LCC TT160 (ebook) |
   DDC 745.5–dc23
LC record available at https://lccn.loc.gov/2020006092
LC ebook record available at https://lccn.loc.gov/2020006093

© 2021 Bearport Publishing Company. All rights reserved. No part of this publication may be reproduced in whole or in part, stored in any retrieval system, or transmitted in any form or by any means, electronic, mechanical, photocopying, recording, or otherwise, without written permission from the publisher.

For more information, write to Bearport Publishing, 5357 Penn Avenue South, Minneapolis, MN 55419. Printed in the United States of America.

Contents

Let's Make Monsters!...................... 4

CREEPY DECORATIONS
Rotting Leaf Zombies 6

CREEPY COSTUME
Horrible, Hairy Werewolf Paws 10

CREEPY TREAT
Sausage Mummies 14

CREEPY FUN
Frankenstein's Monster Piñata..... 18

Frankenstein's Monster................................ 22

Glossary.. 23

Index 24

Read More.. 24

Learn More Online 24

About the Author....................................... 24

Let's Make Monsters!

Let's get ready to make some creepy monsters! This book shows you how to make the following:

◀ **Decaying**, drooling **zombie** leaf **decorations**

A pair of hairy **werewolf** paws for a creepy **costume** ▶

◀ Delicious, funny sausage mummy **treats**

A Frankenstein's monster **piñata** that is fun to make and to smash ▶

Give it a try!
If you've never done something like this before, don't be nervous. Just follow the step-by-step instructions and you'll soon be impressing your friends with the things you can make.

Crafting and cooking are fantastic ways to be **creative**.

But you'll enjoy this time much more if you stay safe and follow our top tips for successful creepy crafting.

Get ready to MAKE!

- Read the instructions carefully before starting. If there's anything you don't understand, ask an adult for help.
- Gather your supplies before you begin.

- Cover your work surface with old newspaper or another protective covering.
- Be careful when using sharp objects.
- When your project is complete, recycle any extra paper, cardboard, or packaging. If you have leftover materials, keep them for a future project.

- Clean up when you've finished working.

Get ready to BAKE!

- Always wash your hands with soap and hot water before you start baking.

- Make sure your work surface and supplies are clean.
- Carefully read the **recipe** before you begin. If there's a step you don't understand, ask an adult for help.
- Gather all your supplies before you start.
- Carefully measure your **ingredients**. Your baking will be more successful if you use exactly the right amount.

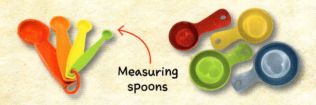

Measuring spoons

- Ask an adult for help when using the oven.
- Clean up and put things away when you've finished baking.

CREEPY DECORATIONS
Rotting Leaf Zombies

Their skin is rotting and sometimes an arm or leg drops right off. What are these frightening, decaying creatures? Zombies! A zombie is a dead person that has come back to life. So what could be better for creepy zombie decorations than rotting leaves?

YOU WILL NEED
- Dead leaves
- Paints and paintbrushes
- Wax paper
- White glue
- Water
- A measuring cup
- A small bowl and spoon
- Scissors
- Colored yarn
- A long ribbon or piece of string
- Clear tape

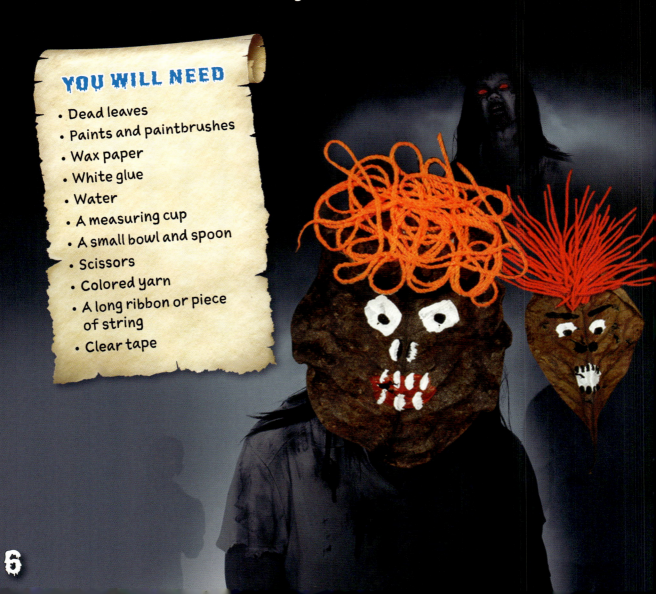

Go on a leaf hunt in a park or your backyard. Try to find large, dead leaves.

If your leaves are damp, allow them to dry for about 24 hours.

 To turn a leaf into a zombie face, paint on eyes, eyebrows, a nose, and a mouth. You can make up your own zombie faces or copy the faces in this book.

Leave an empty space at the top of each face so you can add some hair.

 If you want, paint some red, bloody drool on your zombie's mouth—just as if it's been feasting on brains!

To give your zombie leaves scary hair, lay them on a sheet of wax paper. Next, mix ½ cup of white glue with ½ cup of water in a small bowl or container.

 If you want a zombie leaf to have some crazy hair that stands on end, cut some yarn into 1 inch (2.5 cm) pieces.

 Dip a yarn strand into the glue mixture so it is completely soaked. Then, carefully lay the strand so half of it is on the zombie leaf's forehead and half hangs off the edge of the leaf.

Add as many strands as you want and then leave to dry for 24 hours. As the glue dries, the strands of yarn will become hard.

Use damp paper towels or a wet wash cloth to wipe your hands when they get sticky.

 To give a zombie leaf tangled, messy hair, take a long strand of yarn and completely soak it in the glue mixture.

Next, press one end of the yarn onto the zombie's forehead. Then, twirl and twist the yarn at the top of the zombie's head.

It's fine if some of the yarn goes over the edge of the leaf.

7 Keep adding strands of yarn until you're happy with the look. Leave to dry for 24 hours so the yarn becomes hard.

8 To turn your zombie leaves into a decoration, tape them to a ribbon or piece of string and hang them up.

Back of zombie leaves

AARRRGGHH! IT'S THE ATTACK OF ZOMBIE LEAVES!

Horrible, Hairy Werewolf Paws

A full moon rises in the night sky, and something strange is happening to you. *Hooowl!* You're becoming a werewolf! According to **legends**, a werewolf is a person who becomes half wolf during a full moon. And what does every werewolf need to go hunting? A pair of paws with long, sharp claws.

YOU WILL NEED

- A sheet of thin cardboard
- A pencil
- An adult helper
- Scissors
- 4 sheets of brown felt
- White chalk or a white marker
- Straight pins
- A needle and thread
- Fake fur
- White glue or fabric glue
- A small piece of wax paper
- 1 sheet of yellow foam board

10

To make the gloves for your werewolf paws, begin by making a cardboard template. Ask an adult to place their hand on the cardboard and spread out their fingers and thumb.

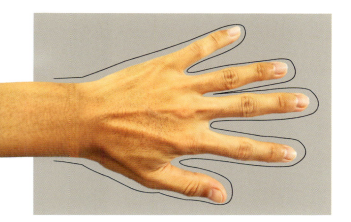

Draw around the hand with a pencil. Cut out the cardboard template.

Draw the fingers slightly wider and longer than in real life. This will give you extra felt to make the sewing easier.

 Lay the cardboard hand onto a piece of felt and carefully pin it in place. Draw around the template using chalk or a white marker. Repeat three more times so you have four felt hand shapes. Carefully cut them out.

 To make one glove, put two felt hand shapes together. Make sure the thumbs are lined up and that any chalk marks are on the sides facing out. Carefully pin the two felt hands together.

Make sure the pins aren't too close to the edges.

11

Sew the two pieces of felt together, keeping your stitches as close to the edges as possible. Be careful not to poke yourself.

Don't worry if your stitches aren't neat! They won't show on the finished gloves.

 When you have sewn the two pieces of felt together, remove the pins and turn the glove inside out.

Glove partly turned inside out

You can use the eraser end of a pencil to gently push out and shape the fingers.

 Repeat steps 3–5 to make a second glove.

12

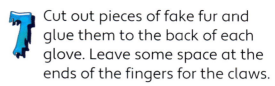 Cut out pieces of fake fur and glue them to the back of each glove. Leave some space at the ends of the fingers for the claws.

 Lay the piece of wax paper on top of the claw shape on this page. Trace the shape onto the wax paper with a pencil. Cut out the template.

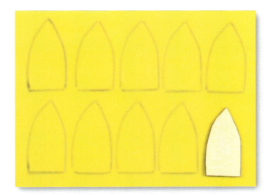

Place the claw template onto the foam board and draw around it. Repeat 9 more times and then cut out your 10 claws.

 Finally, glue the claws to the ends of the fingers and thumbs, and then allow all the glue on the gloves to dry.

YOUR CREEPY WEREWOLF PAWS ARE READY TO WEAR AND SCARE!

CREEPY TREAT
Sausage Mummies

In ancient Egypt, the bodies of the dead were wrapped in cloth and made into **mummies.** However, some movies tell the stories of evil mummies that come back to life. No one wants to meet a monster mummy, but everyone will like these sausage mummies! And they taste so good—there's no way these mummies will be around forever!

INGREDIENTS
- 1 tablespoon honey
- 1 tablespoon ketchup
- 12 precooked sausages
- 1 can crescent roll dough (enough to make 6 rolls)
- 24 edible candy eyeballs

1. Preheat the oven to 350°F (180°C). Line the baking sheet with parchment paper.

2. In a small bowl, mix the honey and ketchup together. Then, brush each sausage with a thin layer of the honey and ketchup mixture.

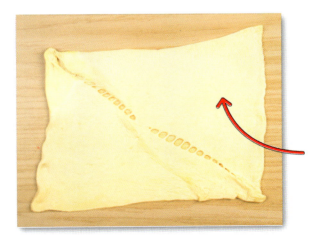

3. Open the can of crescent rolls and carefully unroll the dough. There should be three rectangles of dough inside.

Dough rectangle

The dough rectangles will have lines with small slits across them. With your fingers, gently squeeze the dough together to close up the slits.

Next, cut each rectangle into strips, lengthwise. Each strip should be about ½ inch (1.3 cm) wide.

Take one strip of dough and a sausage. Carefully wrap the dough strip around the sausage. Add a second strip of dough if needed to cover the sausage.

The dough strip will stick to the honey and ketchup coating on the sausage.

Leave a space here for the mummy's eyes.

Place the sausage mummies on the baking sheet. Ask an adult to help you put the sheet into the oven and bake for about 20 minutes.

The mummies are done baking when the dough has turned a light brown color.

Ask an adult to remove the sheet from the oven and set it on a potholder to cool.

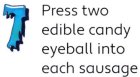 Press two edible candy eyeball into each sausage mummy.

 If you wish, you can drizzle your mummies with some ketchup to add a delicious, gory finishing touch!

THEY ARE ANCIENT. THEY ARE CREEPY. AND THEY ARE THE MOST DELICIOUS MONSTERS YOU WILL EVER EAT!

CREEPY FUN

Frankenstein's Monster Piñata

Everyone loves smashing a **piñata** to get to the treats inside. You can make your own green-skinned monster piñata with a large cereal box and lots of green tissue paper. And then it's time to get smashing!

YOU WILL NEED

- A large, empty cereal box
- Scissors
- Masking tape
- Ribbon or string
- Candy or treats
- A ruler
- 12 large sheets of green tissue paper
- A glue stick
- 2 sheets of black felt
- 1 sheet of white felt
- Aluminum foil

See page 22 for the story behind Frankenstein's monster!

Carefully pull open the edges of the cereal box so it will lay flat. Then, carefully cut off all the flaps as shown.

 Now, reassemble your box. First, tape all the flaps back onto the box using small pieces of masking tape, spaced about 1 inch (2.5 cm) apart. This will make the box break easily when it is hit.

 Tape the two long edges back together to make a box shape. Use small pieces of masking tape spaced about 1 inch (2.5 cm) apart.

 Cut a length of ribbon about 3 feet (1 m) long. Ask an adult to help you make two holes in the center of the top flap of the box. Thread the ribbon through the holes so that you will have a long ribbon for hanging your piñata.

Put your candy or treats inside the box. Then, close the top flap of the box and tape it shut as you did the other edges.

 To give your Frankenstein piñata its green skin, cut sheets of green tissue paper into strips that are as long as the front and sides of the box and are about 3 inches (7.5 cm) tall.

Then, create a fringe effect by making cuts in the strips about 2 inches (5 cm) deep and about ½ inch (1.25 cm) apart.

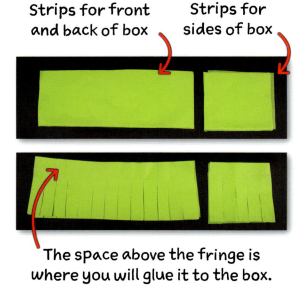

Strips for front and back of box

Strips for sides of box

The space above the fringe is where you will glue it to the box.

 To stick the tissue paper to the box, apply a strip of glue to one side of the box about 3 inches (7.5 cm) from the bottom. Then, press on your first fringed length of tissue paper.

Keep adding rows of tissue paper that slightly overlap until one side is completely covered. Repeat on the other side. Glue the shorter strips to the narrow sides of the box.

Cut two pieces of black felt the size of the top of the box. Cut two slots in one piece of felt to fit around the ribbon and glue this piece to the top of the box.

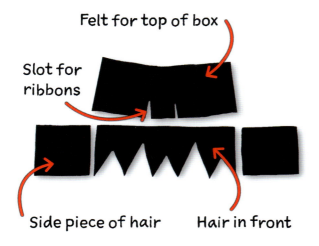

Felt for top of box

Slot for ribbons

Side piece of hair

Hair in front

 Take the second piece of long felt and cut out jagged triangles to make your monster's hair. Glue this piece onto the front of the box. Measure, cut, and glue on two side pieces of hair.

 Cut pieces of black and white felt and glue them onto the box to make a face.

 Crunch up aluminum foil to make two tennis ball-sized lumps. Shape them to look like bolts.

Bolt

Ask an adult to help you make a hole in each side of the box at the bottom. Then, push the bolts into the holes.

YOUR MONSTER PINATA IS READY TO SMASH!

Frankenstein's Monster

This green, groaning monster is a classic costume for Halloween. But where does this terrifying creature come from?

The story of the monster is from a book called *Frankenstein*. It was written in the early 1800s by a British author named Mary Shelley.

In the story, Victor Frankenstein is a scientist who wants to create a man. Victor takes dead bodies and he stitches together different parts to build a giant man. Then, he brings the monster to life. *Eek!*

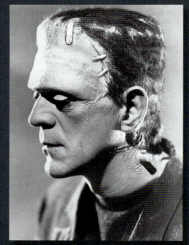

Actor Boris Karloff in the movie *Frankenstein*

The most famous version of the monster appeared in the 1931 movie *Frankenstein*.

A Frankenstein's monster costume

Glossary

decaying rotting or breaking down

ingredients the things that are used to make food

legends stories that have been handed down from the past that may be based on some facts but cannot be proven true

mummies the preserved bodies of dead people or animals, often wrapped in strips of cloth

A mummy cat

piñata a decorated container, often in the shape of an animal, that contains candy and is hung up so blindfolded children can break it open by hitting it with sticks

recipe a set of instructions for making a dish or type of food

werewolf a person who temporarily changes into a wolf or wolflike creature

zombie a dead, decaying body that rises out of its grave

Index

costume 4, 10–13, 22
Egyptian mummies 14
Frankenstein's monster piñata 4, 18–21
Frankenstein's monster 4, 18, 22
ingredients 5, 14
recipe 5

safety 4–5
sausage mummies 14–17
werewolf paws 4, 10–13
werewolves 10
zombie leaves 4, 6–9
zombies 6

Read More

Garbot, Dave. *Mean 'n' Messy Monsters (Cartooning for Kids!)*. Minneapolis: Lerner (2014).

Pearson, Marie. *Frankenstein's Monster (Monster Histories)*. North Mankato, MN: Capstone Press (2020).

Reid, Emily. *Monster Claymation (Claymation Sensation)*. New York: Rosen Publishing (2017).

Learn More Online

1. Go to www.factsurfer.com
2. Enter "**Monsters Crafts**" into the search box.
3. Click on the cover of this book to see a list of websites.

About the Author

Ruth Owen has been developing and writing children's books for more than 10 years. She lives in Cornwall, England, just minutes from the ocean. Ruth loves crafting and is always on the lookout for objects and materials that can be recycled and turned into something new—such as a creepy Halloween costume!